Dear Lady E

MW01012810

The Role of the Woman in the Plan of God.

By:

Judy Seligman

Table of Contents

"Older women likewise are to be reverent in their behavior, not malicious gossips, nor enslaved to much wine, teaching what is good, that they may encourage the younger women to love their husbands, to love their children, to be sensible, pure, workers at home, kind, being subject to their own husbands, that the word of God may not be dishonored."
Titus 2:3–5

Dear Lady Elect,

I am writing to you because it is my heart's desire that you find God in your relationship with your husband. My own ignorance of the Word of God and its application has caused me more grief in my marriage relationship than you could imagine. But, thank God we learn from our mistakes. Ps. 119:71 tells us, "It is good for me that I have been afflicted; that I may learn thy statutes." I hope I can spare you some grief by sharing with you what I have learned.

Our success in our marriages does not depend on where our husbands are with God; it depends on where we are with God. Personally, God has taught me more when my husband was disobedient to the Word (1 Pet. 3:1) than when he was right on. These lessons I hope to share with you in my letters.

For a long time, I have mulled over where to begin to share the principles God has taught me. Since our relationship with God begins with the cross of Christ, so does our relationship with our husbands. Forgiveness of sins is the first matter about which I want to write to you. We have to accept forgiveness for our failures every day. We have to start each day not carrying with us the burden of yesterday's mistakes. I habitually consider Christ crucified and consider the forgiveness of sins He bought for us by His death. Not to accept forgiveness is to think lightly of what Christ did for us. No matter how often or how grievously we've failed, we can start over clean because Christ died for our sins.

Many times, it has been hard for me to accept or even to see my own failures. Consequently, I would blame my worry, fear, temper, resentment, lack of love, etc., etc., etc. on my husband and his behavior. It was a hard pill to swallow, but I had to accept responsibility before God for me — not him. No matter how wrong he was, God held me responsible for my own actions, and not only my actions, but my heart attitudes. These actions and attitudes were sins. My husband's sins may have appeared more grievous, but Christ had to die the same death for my sins of self-pity, self-righteousness and worry as for his blatant sins. (Meditating on the cross kept me aware of this.)

I always tried to urge my husband to change his ways, and it was *never* well received by him. During one of these tearful encounters, the story of the woman caught in the act of adultery in John 8 came into my mind, and the words of verse 7 transposed to speak to my heart. 'Are you so sinless that you can cast stones?' Those words shut my mouth. I realized that I had to overcome my sins of self-pity and self-righteousness before I could criticize my husband's life (2 Cor. 10:6.) I can't tell you in words how that day, over ten years ago, changed my life and my relationship with my husband. It took a lot of pressure off him, because I had to quit nagging him; but more importantly, it changed me. I had to learn to trust Christ to work in my life.

Up to this point in my life, all my efforts were directed at changing my husband, but I was getting nowhere. Now I found out that I was the one who needed to change.

Have you ever tried to change your ways? For example: Have you ever felt really sorry for yourself and your lot in life and tried to change the way you felt? Or, have you ever been depressed and had people tell you to snap out of it? It is impossible. You just can't do it. I couldn't do it either. If there was going to be any change in my life, I realized that God was going to have to do it.

That day, in the face of my sins and weaknesses, the only thing I could do was to confess before God that I had sinned, and I had to believe that Christ loved me and gave Himself for me. After I confessed my sins, not only was I forgiven, but I received a cleansing in my soul that freed me from the power these sins had over me (1 Jo. 1:9.) Little did I know that I had to be set free in order to help my husband toward his freedom. (We'll talk about that at a later date.)

Please read 1 Corinthians 13:1–7. This is the standard that God has set up for us to live; and if we don't, the Word says, "I am nothing." God hasn't just left us with an unreachable standard. He has given us His Holy Spirit to live within us and fulfill for us what He commands of us (Jo. 14:17.) Think about this and we'll talk next month.

Love,

Judy

Scripture references:

• Psalm 119:71 It is good for me that I was afflicted, That I may learn Your statutes.

• 1 Peter 3:1 In the same way, you wives, be submissive to your own husbands so that even if any of them are disobedient to the word, they may be won without a word by the behavior of their wives.

• 2 Corinthians 10:6 And we are ready to punish all disobedience, whenever your obedience is complete.

• 1 John 1:9 If we confess our sins, He is faithful and righteous to forgive us our sins and to cleanse us from all unrighteousness.

• 1 Corinthians 13:1-7 If I speak with the tongues of men and of angels, but have not love, I am become sounding brass, or a clanging cymbal. And if I have the gift of prophecy and know all mysteries and all knowledge; and if I have all faith, so as to remove mountains, but have not love, I am nothing. And if I bestow all my goods to feed the poor, and if I give my body to be burned, but have not love, it profits me nothing. Love suffers long and is kind; love envies not; love parades not itself, is not puffed up, does not behave rudely, seeks not its own, is not provoked, thinks no evil; rejoices not in unrighteousness, but rejoices with the truth; bears all things, believes all things, hopes all things, endures all things.

• John 14:17 even the Spirit of truth: whom the world cannot receive; for it beholds Him not, neither knows him: you know Him; for He abides with you and shall be in you.

August 1988

Letter 1 ~ Questions

- What is the basis for our relationship with God?

- When and how did your relationship with Jesus Christ begin?

- Why are worry, self-pity, fear and resentment sin?

- How is a person freed from these sins?

- Why does your relationship with Christ have to be right before you can have a right relationship with others?

Notes:

Dear Lady Elect,

How are you this month? How is your husband? I pray for you, and I hope you ask God to make you the 'help meet' God ordained you to be for your husband (Gen. 2:18.) Your husband needs you more than either of you realize.

Last month I told you how God convicted me of my sins; and how, through this, He taught me to be quiet and not to speak to my husband concerning his faults.

Soon after that day a friend of mine called me and read me a little poem/prayer. I don't remember it exactly, but it basically was a prayer asking God to put four gates on our lips (Psalm 141:3.) Nothing was to pass through our lips that couldn't pass the test of these four gates: The first gate was, 'Is it truth?' The second was, 'Is it edifying?' The third gate, 'Is it kind?' And the final gate, 'Does it encourage?' This is similar to the passage in Ephesians 4:29

God didn't waste any time in putting these gates to the test in my life. Soon my husband stood before me not in the best of spirits. What I had to say to him may have been true by sight, but it was far from kind, edifying and encouraging. My words could not pass through these gates and my mouth was shut again.

I must admit, as I became quieter, I feared that my husband would think I approved of his behavior, and he would have no incentive to change. But on the contrary, I soon discovered that when I quit arguing with him, he became convicted of his sins by God. He had to face his sins head-on instead of justifying himself by arguing with me. I learned to trust God in a new way.

God was beginning to teach me how important it was for a woman to be quiet. 1 Peter 3:1 tells us that our husbands will be won 'without a word.' This may not seem important to you now, but there is great power in a woman to whom God has taught discretion.

 Last month I said we'd talk about 1 Corinthians 13:1–7. Have you read it yet? This is a very popular portion of scripture. It is read at weddings, and it has been written into song. However, God desires it to be written on our hearts.

The first time I read it was in the Revised Standard Version of the Bible. The words pierced my heart that said, "love is patient... does not insist on its own way... is not irritable or resentful... bears [and] believes all things." My love for my husband fell short at every point. It became obvious to me that resentment, impatience, etc. were my reactions when I loved my husband, and he didn't love me back in the way I wanted to be loved.

God was calling me to love my husband without my expecting to be loved in return. This is exactly opposite of the natural love people have for each other. Some people love and love and can bear a lot of rejection, but eventually they reach an end. Their love cannot 'bear all things.'

This is where I was when God began to work a miracle in me. I was at the end of myself. I said to myself, "Here I am a Christian, and I can't even love my husband." I then prayed, "Lord, if you are in me, and you love my husband; you are going to have to do the loving for me."

I soon found out how real Christ was within me and how much He loved my husband, even in his sins. I learned this because Christ took possession of my heart and loved my husband through me.

When I found myself resentful or impatient, I'd turn to God for forgiveness. I soon discovered that there was two of me. The *old me* for whom Christ died, who could not love (Rom. 6:6) and the new me that was one with God and His love (1 Cor. 6:17.) It took a while, but as the old me decreased, Christ increased in the new me (Jo. 3:30.) As God loved my husband through me, I was so filled with the love of God that the longing I had within me to be loved was satisfied by God. I found I was able to love without needing to be loved in return. God derives satisfaction from the pure act of loving, and God was teaching me to do the same. Later, being loved back became an added blessing, but it was not necessary for my innermost contentment.

One day, some time later, my husband said to me, "I'm so glad you love me." I thought, "You're glad... I'm glad. It is so much easier to live being filled with love instead of being filled with resentment and anger." Jesus did say, "My yoke is easy..." didn't He?

I hope that these letters are encouraging you in your marriage. If you disagree with me or have any problem understanding the principles, I'm trying to share with you, please take it to God. I know He loves you, and He has a special plan for you so that you can know Him personally. Ask God? I know He will answer your prayers.

Love,

Judy

Scripture references:

• Psalm 141:3 Set a guard, O LORD, over my mouth; Keep watch over the door of my lips.

• Ephesians 4:29 Let no unwholesome word proceed from your mouth, but only such a word as is good for edification according to the need of the moment, so that it will give grace to those who hear.

• 1 Cor. 13: 1-7 If I speak with the tongues of men and of angels, but do not have love, I have become a noisy gong or a clanging cymbal. If I have *the gift of* prophecy and know all mysteries and all knowledge; and if I have all faith, so as to remove mountains, but do not have love, I am nothing. And if I give all my possessions to feed *the poor,* and if I surrender my body to be burned, but do not have love, it profits me nothing. Love is patient, love is kind *and* is not jealous; love does not brag *and* is not arrogant, does not act unbecomingly; it does not seek its own, is not provoked, does not take into account a wrong *suffered,* does not rejoice in unrighteousness, but rejoices with the truth; bears all things, believes all things, hopes all things, endures all things.

• Romans 6:6 Knowing this, that our old self was crucified with Him, in order that our body of sin might be done away with, so that we would no longer be slaves to sin;

• 1 Cor. 6:17 But the one who joins himself to the Lord is one spirit with Him.

• John 3:30 He must increase, but I must decrease.

• Galatians 2:20 I have been crucified with Christ; and it is no longer I who live, but Christ lives in me; and the life which I now live in the flesh I live by faith in the Son of God, who loved me and gave Himself up for me.

September 1988

Letter 2 ~ Questions

- How does being quiet display our faith in God?

- Is God's love enough to satisfy the longing in your soul to be loved? Why? or Why not?

- Many believers, after they are saved, try to clean up their acts by giving up sinful habits and obeying the commands of the Word of God. Why is this wrong?

- What is Paul telling us in Galatians 2:20? How does this affect our relationships?

Notes:

Dear Lady Elect,

Families are under attack today as they never have been before. I hope you realize that the problems we go through are really spiritual battles which we have to fight in order to save our homes. There are times I feel more like GI Joe than a wife and a mother. I think you know what I mean.

We've all been wounded in these battles that take place on the home front. That is why, today, I want to touch on one of the foundational stones of a strong, unconquerable marriage: forgiveness.

'Forgive and forget' — One day these words continually pounded my mind. 'Forgive and forget.' They were there at every turn, in every thought, and with everything I did. 'Forgive and forget, forgive and forget.' I finally had to admit to myself that if I could possibly forgive my husband for the many times he hurt and disappointed me, I would find it impossible to forget them.

How could I forget? The memory of the past still had the power to pierce my heart and tear my eyes. I had been wounded in battle. They (whoever 'they' are) say that time heals all wounds, but it really doesn't. Instead, the pains in life get buried in our soul only to surface when they are brought to mind or when we're hurt again.

The longer we're married, the more the wounds multiply. Eventually our self-defense mechanisms are triggered, and we build walls to protect ourselves from being hurt again. I know a woman who had a wall of defense built so high around herself that it could be felt by all who knew her. She built this spiritual wall because of a bad marriage, and she was determined never to be hurt again.

These walls that we build help to keep pain out; but unfortunately, these walls keep God and others out too. They also keep us from being one with our husbands as God intended us to be.

'Forgive and forget' —I wanted to forgive but how could I forget when the pain still was fresh within me, and I was afraid of being hurt again. The answer was in the Word of God.

The Bible tells us that God said, "I will forgive their wickedness and will remember their sins no more (Hebrews 8:12)." God, who knows all and whose heart has been wounded by the sins of mankind, not only forgives but forgets also.

When we sin, God the Father doesn't look at our sins but at His Son, Jesus. When Christ died, our sins were placed on Him, not on us. He died and paid the debt we owed for our sins. God doesn't look at us but at His Son, and He forgives and forgets and 'remembers our sins no more.'

King David said in Psalm 32:2, "How blessed is the man to whom the Lord does not impute (charge to his account) iniquity (sins)." God does not charge our sins to our account because He imputed them to Christ 2000 years ago. We are completely free from the debt of our sins, because it was paid by Jesus on the cross.

This same principle can empower us to 'forgive and forget' because Christ did not die just for our sins but for all the sins of the world (2 Corinthians 5:19; 1 John 2:2). I learned to 'forgive and forget' by appropriating what Christ did for me and my husband. I couldn't forgive my husband because he deserved forgiveness, but by looking upon Christ crucified, I could forgive him, not for his sake, but for Christ's sake (Ephesians 4:32.) I could forgive my husband even if he never asked to be forgiven or said he was sorry.

Instead of keeping a record book against my husband of all the pain he caused me, I had to look at Christ and know that the ledger was cleared for him. There was no debt on my husband's account because Christ's death paid it.

I can't tell you how important it is to forgive. There cannot be any healing, restoration, salvation, or deliverance, if unforgiveness is present in your relationships. If you have hurts that cause you to hold on to unforgiveness, do not allow them to be buried. Deal with them today! If you can't forgive, go to God and confess your unforgiveness. Christ has accomplished everything needed to empower you to forgive; be open to God.

Forgiveness has brought me freedom: freedom from the past for the present, and I don't have to worry about the future. When offenses happen (and they always will), there is more than enough grace from Christ's cross to cover them. What is grace but undeserved mercy and forgiveness. We receive it for our own lives, and from the same source, the cross of Christ, we can give it to others.

Please let go of past hurts; release forgiveness and let God heal your soul and relationship. Start each day fresh and look at your husband in the same way. Keep your focus on Christ and 'forgive and forget' for the sake of Jesus Christ. Ask God. He'll teach you how.

Love,

Judy

Scripture references:

• Psalm 32:2 How blessed is the man to whom the LORD does not impute iniquity, and in whose spirit there is no deceit!

• 2 Corinthians 5:19 Namely, that God was in Christ reconciling the world to Himself, not counting their trespasses against them, and He has committed to us the word of reconciliation.

• 1 John 2:2 He Himself is the propitiation for our sins; and not for ours only, but also for those of the whole world.

• Ephesians 4:32 Be kind to one another, tender-hearted, forgiving each other, just as God in Christ also has forgiven you.

October 1988

Letter 3 ~ Questions

- Holding on to past hurts paralyzes us as a Christian. Why?

- Why should sins committed against us never be communicated to others?

- What should you do when past hurts come to mind?

- How does forgiving someone who hurt you prove your loyalty to the Cross of Christ?

Notes:

Dear Lady Elect,

Today I want to share with you one of the most freeing revelations I have ever received about the nature and the power of God.

Did you know that in our lives God has complete control over every detail no matter how large or small, and He loves us so much that He is working all things that happen to us for our ultimate good (Rom. 8:28)?

There is a scripture in the Word of God that commands us, "in everything give thanks" (1 Thessalonians 5:18). There isn't any way we could do this if God weren't in total control. We've been taught to give God thanks for our blessings, but if we're to give Him thanks for 'everything' that would include the negative things that happen to us as well as the positive. The only way we can possibly thank God for 'all things' is if we really believe that God loves us and has a purpose for all the details in our lives, both good and bad.

One of the most negative moments in the history of mankind, the crucifixion of the Son of God, was the source of the world's greatest blessings. Things aren't always the way they seem to be.

Have you ever read the book of Job? In the beginning of the account, Job was a very prosperous man with many servants, herds, and a large family. God was pleased with His servant, Job. Satan approached God and accused Job before Him. Satan said that the only reason that Job worshipped God was because of all the blessings God had given to him. If Job's blessings were removed, Satan had determined that Job would curse God. In order to touch Job, Satan had to have God's permission. God set limits to Job's trial, and Satan wasn't allowed to do anything to Job outside the limits that God had set.

The point I am trying to make is this, like Job, nothing can happen to us unless God permits it, even trials and temptation. First Corinthians 10:13 states that God "will not allow you to be tempted beyond what you are able."

I remember the day that I realized this truth. My husband came home in a terrible mood, both argumentative and abusive. I thought, " God, You have a purpose for this so... I thank You. I thank You for his mood, the turmoil and what you are doing in his life."

Nothing miraculous happened externally; but internally I had peace with God. I knew that God was in control. From then on, I started thanking God when I didn't understand what was going on in my life, knowing He was in charge.

God does a lot of tearing down and disciplining in us in order to work out His will in our lives. As I started to trust God and to thank Him for His loving control, it got me out of the way, while He worked. God was now allowed to tear down and discipline. He now had freedom to work in me and my husband.

Guess what else it did? It made me quieter. I quit complaining and murmuring to my husband, and I looked more and more to God. Peace took possession of my heart. God produced a strong, quiet confidence within me. Everyone noticed it. It wasn't natural; it was supernatural. It was from God.

I know that anyone, who will dare to believe God, can have this strength. Will you believe Him? I was thinking yesterday that God loves me as if I were His only child, and all His forces in the universe are working together just for me. I know I'm not His only child, but He loves me just as if I were. He loves you in the same way, and He is working all the things in your life for your good. Please trust God and start now to thank Him in everything.

Love,

Scripture references:

• Romans 8:28 And we know that God causes all things to work together for good to those who love God, to those who are called according to His purpose.

• 1 Thessalonians 5:18 In everything give thanks; for this is God's will for you in Christ Jesus.

• 1 Corinthians 10:13 No temptation has overtaken you, but such as is common to man; and God is faithful, who will not allow you to be tempted beyond what you are able, but with the temptation will provide the way of escape also, so that you will be able to endure.

November 1988

Letter 4 ~ Questions

- Is complaining about our life sin?   Why?

- Does the belief in the sovereignty of God affect your life on a daily basis?

- Why is the doctrine of sovereignty crucial to our spiritual life?

Notes:

Dear Lady Elect,

In October's letter we spoke a little about our being in warfare. Unfortunately, most people don't know who their real enemy is, and they end up fighting the wrong things. We hear of wars against poverty, drug abuse, pornography, alcohol abuse; and yet, the pornography goes on, the drug abuse increases, etc. On the personal level, we often get into battles with our husbands, children, friends, and families. We can't change anyone. We seem to be fighting losing battles.

One of the reasons we're defeated so often is because we're fighting visible, temporal things when our real enemy is the power behind these evils. Ephesians 6:12 states that "we do not wrestle against flesh and blood but against principalities, against powers, against the rulers of the darkness of this age, against spiritual hosts of wickedness in the heavenly places." This scripture tells us that, behind the scene of flesh and blood, there are invisible powers who are our actual enemies.

Before the creation of man, when Satan was cast out of heaven, he took one-third of the angels with him. He was given, as his domain the 'air' that surrounds the earth (Eph. 2:2.) Having only 'air' with which to work, he has been able to control the entire world system by means of thought projections. By projecting thoughts into the minds of men and women, Satan has 'deceived the whole world' (Rev.12:9) and has brought it under his power. First John 5:19 tells us, "We know that we are of God, and the whole world lies under the sway of the wicked one."

This is why, as Christians, the Word of God is so important to us. It is the only thing on this planet that has not been tainted with Satan's lies. We have all been deceived into believing the thoughts projected into our minds by Satan. The only way we can discern what is truth and what is not is to weigh our thoughts against the Word of God. If they are contrary to what we read there, we have to question where these thoughts have originated.

For instance, let's say you committed a sin and later confessed it to God; yet, you were constantly hounded by guilt. Romans 8:1 in the Bible states, "There is therefore now no condemnation for those who are in Christ Jesus." Knowing this, you would have to cast down the guilty thoughts as being projected to you by Satan's demons and begin to believe the truth of God's Word by accepting the forgiveness that is yours freely through Christ's death on the cross.

I know that I was always personally plagued with financial worries. In my thoughts I constantly worried about how I was going to pay my bills. This time of year, Christmas, was a particularly worrisome one for me. One day, though, I read Matthew 6 in which

Jesus was telling his disciples that their heavenly Father loved them and would provide them with their earthly needs. In verses 33 and 34 He told them, "Seek first His (God's) Kingdom and His righteousness; and all these things shall be added to you. Therefore, do not be anxious for tomorrow: for tomorrow will care for itself. Each day has enough trouble of its own." With these words I realized that I didn't have to worry. I didn't have to receive the worrisome thoughts that were projected into my mind. After that time, when worry would come to me, as it always did, I would just remind myself that I had a Father in heaven who knew all my needs and would provide for me. Through this, I gained peace of mind. And guess what? My Father in heaven has always been faithful to provide for all my needs over the years, sometimes miraculously.

Because of these principles, I urge you to read your Bible. We can't fight thought projections without knowing the truth. I know that if you are not a reader, the Bible may seem overwhelming to you. May I offer you some suggestions? First, pray to God to help you. His Holy Spirit is within you to assist you. Start in the New Testament and read only a little each day. God will open up your understanding. Pray, also, that God would direct you to a place where His Word is taught. This will be the beginning of the defeat of Satan in your life. (Please read 2 Corinthians 10:3–5.)

Next month we'll talk further on spiritual warfare.

Love,

Judy

Scripture references:

• Ephesians 6:12 For our struggle is not against flesh and blood, but against the rulers, against the powers, against the world forces of this darkness, against the spiritual forces of wickedness in the heavenly places.

• Ephesians 2:2 In which you formerly walked according to the course of this world, according to the prince of the power of the air, of the spirit that is now working in the sons of disobedience.

• 1 John 5:19 We know that we are of God, and that the whole world lies in the power of the evil one.

• Romans 8:1 Therefore there is now no condemnation for those who are in Christ Jesus.

• Matthew 6:33-34 But seek first His kingdom and His righteousness, and all these things will be added to you. So do not worry about tomorrow; for tomorrow will care for itself. Each day has enough trouble of its own.

• 2 Corinthian 10:3-6 For though we walk in the flesh, we do not war according to the flesh, for the weapons of our warfare are not of the flesh, but divinely powerful for the destruction of fortresses. *We are* destroying speculations and every lofty thing raised up against the knowledge of God, and *we are* taking every thought captive to the obedience of Christ, and we are ready to punish all disobedience, whenever your obedience is complete.

December 1988

Letter 5 ~ Questions

• Where do thoughts of worry and anxiety originate?

• How does the Word of God combat these thoughts?

• Is it possible, with God, to live a worry-free life?

Notes:

Dear Lady Elect,

Last month I promised you that we'd continue to talk about spiritual warfare, especially as it applies to women.

Satan's first attack against women was in the Garden of Eden. Scripture tells us that Eve fell in the garden because she was completely deceived by the serpent. Adam fell, not because of deception, but because of his desire to please his wife. Eve looked at the tree of which God told her not to eat and "saw that the tree was good..." (Genesis 3:6.) She was totally deceived into thinking something that was evil was actually good.

Women today are being deceived in the same way. One of the things that God has taught me in my marriage is not to trust in my inherent sense of right and wrong. No matter how right I think I am or how sure I am that I know what is best for my family, I have learned not to trust in these feelings. I, like Eve, may be deceived into thinking something 'evil' is 'good.' Proverbs 3:5 tells us to "Trust in the Lord with all your heart and lean not on your own understanding." I had to learn to trust God.

After the fall in Genesis 3:15, God put enmity (warfare) between Satan and the woman. In order to protect her from Satan, in Genesis 3:16, God placed the woman under the authority of her husband. All decisions were to be made through him, thus protecting the family from being deceived through the woman.

Today, more than ever, the woman is being attacked, and Satan is drawing her out from under the covering God has provided for her. If a woman leaves the provision made by God for her protection, she is open to demonic attack and deception.

I know that this is not a popular stand to take in this day of women's liberation, and I can almost hear the cries of protest as I write. But, if women would remove the blinders from their eyes, they would see the inroads Satan has made in this age: rampant divorce, sexual immorality, spoiled-rebellious children, drug and alcohol abuse, etc. These evils are growing hand-in-hand with the current trend in America toward women's liberation. Satan promises a woman independence and freedom, but his underlying motive is stated in John 10:10. He comes to rob, kill, and destroy.

I've been saved seventeen years, and I have seen numerous Christian women innocently drawn out from under the coverings of their husbands and into the world where their faith in Christ and marriages were destroyed. If I could stand on a roof top and shout, I would cry out to women to pray to God to show them their place in the home and how to live out the role God designed for them to the fullest. This is where God's grace is for a woman.

I know that there are exceptions to God's norms, but they are exceptions. I also don't want to place anyone under condemnation. I only ask that you turn to God, be open, and ask Him to teach you. If you've failed, confess your sins and commit yourself to God right where you are, and trust Him to work everything, even your failures, for good (Romans 8:28.) He will answer you!

Jesus came to set us free (John 8:32, 36.) Through His death on the cross, He has freed us from our sins and eternal damnation. He has also won for us victory over Satan, so we can be free from his dominion. This victory begins to be realized in our marriage as we arrange ourselves in Godly order under our husbands. In this order, we are not only protected from demonic deception, but God can bring His resurrection life into our homes.

Personally, for my husband and myself, after twenty-one years of marriage, there is now more love and excitement in our relationship than when we were newlyweds. This flame was rekindled when God showed me my place under my husband. The Holy Spirit has kept that flame strong and warm even through times when most women would have called it quits.

I have also heard countless testimonies from other women who have been truly liberated through godly submission. So, I ask you; give God's way a try.

Love,

Judy

Scripture references:

• Genesis 3:6 When the woman saw that the tree was good for food, and that it was a delight to the eyes, and that the tree was desirable to make one wise, she took from its fruit and ate; and she gave also to her husband with her, and he ate.

• Trust in the LORD with all your heart and do not lean on your own understanding.

• Genesis 3:15 And I will put enmity between you and the woman….

• Genesis 3:16 …Yet your desire will be for your husband, and he will rule over you.

• John 10:10 The thief comes only to steal and kill and destroy; I came that they may have life and have it abundantly.

• Romans 8:28 And we know that God causes all things to work together for good to those who love God, to those who are called according to His purpose.

• John 8:32 And you will know the truth, and the truth will make you free.

• John 8:36 So if the Son makes you free, you will be free indeed.

Letter 6 ~ Questions

- Do you believe that you can be deceived into thinking something wrong is the right thing? How does submission protect you from this type of deception?

- How does submission make you free from your husband?

- I would like to challenge you to trust God and to try submission to your husband for one week. If the world doesn't fall apart, try it for another week. I call this 'The Submission Challenge.' Keep a diary of the results.

Notes:

Dear Lady Elect,

Last month in my letter I mentioned submission and the Christian woman. I know that submission is not a popular subject in this day of women's liberation, but its lack of popularity is due to a misunderstanding of its Godly definition.

Most people think that by being submissive a woman is demeaned and considered of lesser value than a man, and it puts her into a position of abject subjugation. This is not true of Godly submission.

First of all, Godly submission is never toward your husband first. It is initially toward God. In the Word, God calls the Christian woman to be submissive to her husband _AS UNTO THE LORD_. I personally, couldn't submit to my husband until, through faith, I mentally put my husband out of the way, so I could see God. Let me explain what I mean.

It all started with my believing Proverbs 21:1. It basically states that God has the heart of the king in His hand and can turn it in any direction He pleases. Practically, this meant for me that God had control of my husband and could turn him in any direction He wanted. By submitting to my husband, I was actually submitting to God who directed his heart.

This is what it means in Ephesians 5:22 where it says "Wives, submit to your own husbands, as to the Lord." I had to quit looking at my husband and trust God who governs through my husband. It was never important where my husband was in his faith, because I wasn't really submitting to him, even if it looked as though I was. I was actually submitting to God.

The occasions are so numerous that it would be impossible for me to list the times God has shown me His reality and faithfulness through submission. Any time my husband made a decision that didn't settle well with me, I'd just go to God and pray. "Lord, if this is not Your will, turn his heart." Through prayer and faith, I've seen the heart of King Husband turn in the Lord's hands. I've seen my husband be so set in his ways and miraculously change his mind. I've seen situations orchestrated by God to cover bad decisions on my husband's part; and I've also seen situations where my husband was right after all; and if I would have had my way, it would have been disastrous.

God started to humble me and teach me submission over twelve years ago, and it has always worked out for my good. Never once have I regretted being submissive. Submission has actually given me independence from my husband by making me dependent on God, not on him. Submission has given me a greater sense of my accountability to God in my marital relationship, because God has called me to submission, trusting Him regardless of where my husband was in his faith. First Peter 3:1 tells us point-blank to be submissive to our husbands who 'obey not the word.' Submission has also made me calm and relaxed in my relationship with my husband. I pray more; argue less.

By trusting God, I can release God's governing power into my home. Please understand, if you are trusting God, He will not let you down. *God* is the One who has placed the man over the woman. *God* is the one who tells us women to be submissive to our husbands. Therefore, *God* has a responsibility toward us to work in our husbands as we submit, trusting Him. First Peter 3:1 even promises us that if we are submissive, our husbands will be won to obedience to the Word of God. I've studied the original Greek from which this passage is translated, and it states that our husbands will definitely be won if we are submissive. God is so faithful to His Word, and over the years He has never let me down in this area.

Did you know that the Word of God does not tell the woman to love her husband? Its only command to her is to submit to him. I have found, though, that it is through submission that a woman walks in the Spirit of God and the fruit of the Spirit is love. Because of this, I am in love with my husband. I love him just the way he is without alterations, and my love for him is always growing stronger.

I am in a position where I've met countless women who confess to me that their natural love for their husbands has grown cold. But I've also seen that as they learn to trust God and grow into submissive wives, God gives them a new heart toward their husbands — one of love and tenderness.

Jesus Christ left His throne in heaven and became a servant (Philippians.2:7–8) to die for our sins and bring redemption into the world. He accomplished as a servant what couldn't be accomplished from the throne. Through God, we as women can bring that power of redemption into our families by dying to self and living a life of submission. Ask God to teach you how. It's never too late. Please! Give God's way a try.

Love,

Judy

• Proverbs 21: 1 The king's heart is like channels of water in the hand of the LORD; He turns it wherever He wishes

• Ephesians 5:22 Wives, be subject to your own husbands, as to the Lord.

• 1 Peter 3:1 In the same way, you wives, be submissive to your own husbands so that even if any of them are disobedient to the word, they may be won without a word by the behavior of their wives.

• Philippians 2:5-8 Have this attitude in yourselves which was also in Christ Jesus, who, although He existed in the form of God, did not regard equality with God a thing to be grasped, but emptied Himself, taking the form of a bond-servant, *and* being made in the likeness of men. Being found in appearance as a man, He humbled Himself by becoming obedient to the point of death, even death on a cross.

Letter 7 ~ Questions

• Why is faith in the sovereignty of God the basis of the doctrine of submission?

• Do you believe that God can govern through your husband? Why or why not?

• Would a man's free will negate or void the sovereignty of God? (Lamentations 3:37)

Notes:

Dear Lady Elect,

Last month we started to talk about Godly submission. This month I hope to clarify its meaning by further explaining the role of a submissive wife.

Submission is not just doing everything your husband tells you to do. (That would be easy.) It is laying down your life and living by the power of God to complement your husband's life.

First Corinthians 11:9 tells us that "man was not created for the woman's sake, but woman for the man's sake." Think about it; you were created for your husband. God also said, "It is not good that the man should be alone; I will make him a help meet for him (Gen. 2:18.)" What these scriptures are telling us is that our husbands need us, and they are incomplete without us. We were made for them, to complete them.

Most women, and I was one of them, think that in marriage their husbands will somehow fulfill them. (I have yet to find a woman who has reached this 'nirvana' in her marriage.) The fact is, the woman was created to fulfill her husband, not vice versa. The woman finds fulfillment by living out the role of 'help meet' for which she was created.

The woman has amazing power in the marriage because of the man's need for her. This power was first demonstrated in the Garden of Eden. Do you realize that Eve was completely deceived into thinking she was doing something good for herself when she ate of the forbidden fruit and offered it to Adam? Adam knew otherwise but still ate of the fruit. First Timothy 2:14 states that the woman was deceived but Adam was not deceived. He knew it was wrong, but he went along with Eve. This demonstrates what great power she had over him.

Because of this power, the Law stated (1 Kings 11:2) that Hebrew men were not allowed to marry pagan women because these women would 'surely', not maybe, lead them astray. After the garden incident, it was obvious that the woman had great power over the man, so God gave this law to protect his people from completely falling away from Him through ungodly women.

However, the power of the woman was not designed to be destructive but was ordained to fulfill the man, win him to Christ, and encourage him in God's will. It is no wonder, in Proverbs 12:4, that this woman is called the 'crown' of her husband.

This role of the wife is defined in 1 Peter 3:1. It reads, "In the same way, you wives, be submissive to your own husbands so that even if any of them are disobedient to the word, they *may be won without a word by the behavior of their wives*." This scripture addresses the women whose husbands 'are disobedient to the word.' This would include all men: the unsaved man, the backslidden man, and the spiritual man who has areas in his life that are not submitted to God's Word. In other words, all men can be won to Christ by their wives.

In submission, the woman directs her attention to her husband as her mission field in order to win him to Christ. Her husband is to be the priority in her life; after all, she was made 'for the man's sake.' This work, however, is not to be carried out through natural means. *Christ is in us* to supply us with all we need. The fruits of the Spirit, in Galatians 5:22–23, are to be poured out on our husbands as we abide in Christ.

If Eve could lead Adam to do something contrary to what he knew was right, the woman with God on her side certainly has the power to turn her husband to God. I can hear you saying, "But you don't know my husband." He is probably described in the words of 1 Peter 3:1, "disobedient to the word." These words are better translated: non-persuadable, stubborn and hard hearted. God knew that words could not win this type of man to the Word, but that the faith and love of a Godly woman could win him '*without a word*' God loves your husband, and He sent His Son to die for him on the cross. He also saw that it wasn't good for him to be alone, so He gave him a godly wife. (That's you!) Christ dwells in your heart so that God can have a means of expressing His love to your husband. Be available to God, and you will see what God will do through you.

My own marriage, at one time, was, to put it mildly, falling apart. By sight, it looked as if I was the innocent victim of a bad relationship. The situation was so unbearable that it put me on my knees before God and then, God began to work *in me*. He had to first remove the log in my eye, so I could help remove the speck in my husband's eye. I assure you, my self-righteousness, ignorance and self-pity formed a huge log. Through the intake of the Word of God and the power of the Holy Spirit within me, I learned to love my husband. I could have walked away, but if I had, I would have forfeited the opportunity I was given to know God and His grace, and to see His faithfulness working on my behalf. I'm so excited about my marriage and what God has done in me and in my husband.

Ask God to give you His heart toward your husband. Make your husband your mission field. As women, this is our calling in life. We can do thousands of things for God; but if we don't live in the will of God and fulfill our roles as wives, all the things we do will add up to nothing on the Judgment Day. Please, seek God in this; your husband's eternity could be at stake.

Love,

Judy

Scripture references:

• 1 Corinthians 11:9 For indeed man was not created for the woman's sake, but woman for the man's sake.

• Genesis 2:18 Then the LORD God said, "It is not good for the man to be alone; I will make him a helper suitable for him."

• 1 Timothy 2:14 And it was not Adam who was deceived, but the woman being deceived, fell into transgression.

• 1 Kings 11: 2 From the nations concerning which the LORD had said to the sons of Israel, "You shall not associate with them, nor shall they associate with you, for they will surely turn your heart away after their gods." Solomon held fast to these in love.

• 1Peter 3:1 In the same way, you wives, be submissive to your own husbands so that even if any of them are disobedient to the word, they may be won without a word by the behavior of their wives.

• Galatians 5:22-23 But the fruit of the Spirit is love, joy, peace, patience, kindness, goodness, faithfulness, gentleness, self-control; against such things there is no law. Now those who belong to Christ Jesus have crucified the flesh with its passions and desires.

March 1989

Letter 8 ~ Questions

• After reading this letter, do you understand why Satan desires to demean or destroy the doctrine of submission? Has he been successful?

• What are the negative results of the women's liberation movement on the married woman as propagated by the world system?

• Why did God ordain that the woman should be submissive to her husband's authority?

Notes:

Dear Lady Elect,

This month I'd like to address the subject of trials, since we all seem to have our fair share of them. Some trials are short, lasting days, weeks, or months. Some are long, lasting for years with no end in sight.

During these times of prolonged trials, no matter what we do or how hard we pray, nothing seems to change. We watch other Christians. We hear testimonies of the way God is working in their lives, but God doesn't seem to hear our prayers. There seems to be no way out for us. One of the greatest temptations during a prolonged trial is to give up on God and make our own way of escape. *Don't do it!* It will only end in futility. You will forfeit the blessings God has planned for you.

I have personally found that the pressures and duration of our trials, though painful, are necessary. Pressure and time turn coal into precious diamonds. In the same manner the time and pressure of trials are necessary to conform us, the coal, into the image of God's precious Son. All that the coal has to do to be changed is to rest in the earth and yield to the pressure. God and *time* will do the rest. It is the same with us. It takes time, but there is no other route to take in order to be transformed.

These times of trials are the most valuable periods in our Christian walk. The greatest saints in the Bible went through prolonged trials. Joseph spent thirteen years as a slave and as a prisoner before God raised him up to rule Egypt. Moses spent forty years in exile tending sheep before God called him to deliver his people. David spent seventeen years hiding in caves before he was made king. John the Baptist lived thirty years in the desert before his public ministry began. I think you get the idea. Times of trials are absolutely necessary for our spiritual growth. God is faithful and will not release us until His work is done in us.

Trials drain us of our natural strength. Here God can bring us to a place where there is nothing and no one to rely on but Him. This is where God can manifest Himself to us. The place of our trials is 'Holy Ground.' Jacob spoke of it in Genesis 28:16–17: "Surely the Lord is in this place, and I did not know it." and "How awesome is this place! This is none other than the house of God, and this is the gate of heaven." Our trials are our gateway into God's presence.

I have recently come through a trial in which God pulled down all the superficial props upon which I leaned. I was taught, through experience, the faithfulness of God. During this time when there were no earthly provisions or comforts, God was there to comfort me and provide for me. The Word of God became alive, and all the promises of the Word became my 'daily bread.' I learned that our afflictions are actually gifts from a God who loves us. I heard that a great saint once said that he 'embraced his chains.' Now I know why. They were his *gateway* into the kingdom of God.

Hebrews 4:11 tells us to "strive to enter... rest." In our trials we have to learn to *rest* in God's love. He loves us, and He wants us to realize His love. His love was expressed to us when He sent His Son to die for us so that nothing could separate us from His love.

Sin cannot separate us from God's love, because Christ bore all our sins in His body, so we could be forgiven (1 Peter 2:24.) Our sinful nature can't separate us because our old nature was crucified with Christ (Romans 6:6.) Finally, Satan cannot separate us because Christ defeated him (Colossians 2:15.) Jesus is now seated at the right hand of the Father with absolute authority over Satan and all his demons (Ephesians 1:20–21.) Therefore, nothing can separate us from the love of God.

We can fellowship with God anytime and anywhere. Instead of spending time worrying about your situation, spend time with God, not just praying but basking in His love. This is your place of rest. Then, when distractions come, and they always do, 'strive' to get back to that place of rest. Cast down the thoughts that stand between you and your place of rest. You'll always find God waiting there to fellowship with you. Establish as your goal to constantly abide in your place of rest, and everything else in your spiritual life will fall into place.

Trust God and come to know Him where you are. He is on the throne. He knows everything that is going on in your life. He is a faithful Father who will provide you with all your physical needs as you seek Him. Accept your trial, and let God and time transform you into the image of His Son.

Love,

Judy

Scripture references:

• Genesis 28:16-17 Then Jacob awoke from his sleep and said, "Surely the LORD is in this place, and I did not know it." He was afraid and said, "How awesome is this place! This is none other than the house of God, and this is the gate of heaven.

• Hebrews 4:11 Therefore let us be diligent to enter that rest, so that no one will fall, through following the same example of disobedience.

• 1 Peter 2:24 And He Himself bore our sins in His body on the cross, so that we might die to sin and live to righteousness; for by His wounds you were healed.

• Colossians 2:15 When He had disarmed the rulers and authorities, He made a public display of them, having triumphed over them through Him.

• Ephesians 1:20-21 Which He brought about in Christ, when He raised Him from the dead and seated Him at His right hand in the heavenly *places,* far above all rule and authority and power and dominion, and every name that is named, not only in this age but also in the one to come.

April 1989

Letter 9 ~ Questions

- Jesus was a man of sorrows, acquainted with grief (Is 53). Yet, He did this without sin. How is His victory transferred to us?

- Does God have a plan in ALL suffering?

- How does God's sovereignty affect your decisions?

Notes:

Dear Lady Elect,

Lately I've been hearing some wonderful testimonies from Godly women. They are seeking God and learning to live out their roles as God has defined them in His Word. In this they are finding peace and contentment. Not only that, but as they are getting to know God, their relationships with their husbands are being renewed. Words cannot express how excited this makes me. It is awesome to see God's Word becoming substance in the lives of these ladies.

Some of the circumstances in which these women are living in are far from ideal. Anyone can be content when things are going well, but God is glorified even more when a woman praises Him in a bad situation. Our contentment and strength during the storms are a witness to all those who know us that God lives. God's strength in troubled times is available to us as we look to Him in faith. Personally, God has always been faithful to me, even when I was faithless. How much more does He uphold us as we cast ourselves into His care? Situations don't always change when we entrust them to God; but as we look to Him, He changes *us* in our situations.

This month I'd like to address those women who are married to unbelievers, the unsaved, carnal, and backslidden, and are trying to raise their children to know God.

The Word of God promises us in 1 Corinthians 7:14 that, if we remain with our unbelieving husbands and do not depart, our children will be sanctified which means to be set apart for God. I know many women who have left their husbands for the sake of their children. In most cases, this is not scriptural. Before my husband was converted, I clung to this scripture as a promise from God. One of the reasons I remained with my husband was because of God's Word. God said my children would be sanctified by my remaining in my situation. He was faithful to keep this promise that He made to me.

The most crucial lesson I learned during this period of my life was the importance of remaining under the authority of my husband, even though he was not walking with the Lord. A fundamental principle of the kingdom of God is that those under authority have authority (Luke 7:6-8.)

A woman under the authority of her husband has authority over her children. If a woman refuses to go under the authority of her husband, she will not have the authority over her children that she needs to train and discipline them.

Even though my husband was usually disinterested in the affairs of our household, I continually asked him for his advice. God, however, did not expect me to trust my husband, but He expected me to trust Him. Before I would go to my husband about a matter, I'd pray to God asking Him to govern through my husband. As we trust in God, He *can* govern and does 'turn the heart of the king' anyway He pleases (Prov. 21:1.)

By not usurping my husband's authority, three primary things were accomplished. First, my husband was built up and encouraged in his Godly role as the head of our household. Second, by my being under my husband's authority, I was endowed with Godly authority that my children honored and obeyed. Third, my children honored their father.

One of the most prevalent problems of American youth is that they are rebellious and lack respect for authority. We can, as submissive wives, build respect for authority in our children. The Word of God has only one primary command for children — "Honor your father and mother" (Eph. 6:2.) We have a great amount of influence on our children in this area of their lives. If we honor their father, they will; if we don't, they won't.

Before I close, I'd like to touch on one more point. The scriptures continually tell us to cover each other's faults and not to expose them. As Christian mothers, we owe it to our family members to cover their sins. As much as was in my power, I hid my husband's lifestyle from the children. I never spoke to them of his faults. When things were unavoidably exposed to them, I would use the opportunity to explain to them the weakness of man and the abundant gift of God when He sent His Son to die for our sins. I encouraged them to forgive and to cover their father as God has forgiven and covered our sins.

I know when you are married to an unbeliever you can feel very alone, but we are not alone. Our Lord has promised us that He will never leave us nor forsake us (Heb. 13:5.) His grace is truly sufficient for us (2 Cor. 12:9.)

Love,

Judy

Scripture references:

• 1 Corinthians 7:14 For the unbelieving husband is sanctified through his wife, and the unbelieving wife is sanctified through her believing husband; for otherwise your children are unclean, but now they are holy.

• Luke 7:6-8 Now Jesus *started* on His way with them; and when He was not far from the house, the centurion sent friends, saying to Him, "Lord, do not trouble Yourself further, for I am not worthy for You to come under my roof; for this reason I did not even consider myself worthy to come to You, but *just* say the word, and my servant will be healed. "For I also am a man placed under authority, with soldiers under me; and I say to this one, 'Go!' and he goes, and to another, 'Come!' and he comes, and to my slave, 'Do this!' and he does it."

• Proverbs 21:1 The king's heart is like channels of water in the hand of the LORD; He turns it wherever He wishes.

• Ephesians 6:2 HONOR YOUR FATHER AND MOTHER (which is the first commandment with a promise).

• Hebrews 13:5   Make sure that your character is free from the love of money, being content with what you have; for He Himself has said, "I WILL NEVER DESERT YOU, NOR WILL I EVER FORSAKE YOU,"

• 2 Corinthians 12:9 And He has said to me, "My grace is sufficient for you, for power is perfected in weakness." Most gladly, therefore, I will rather boast about my weaknesses, so that the power of Christ may dwell in me.

May 1989

Letter 10 ~ Questions

• How are children protected by a woman who lives in submission to her husband?

• What long term affects does respect for authority have on children?

• What do children learn from us as we live out our spiritual lives?

Notes:

Dear Lady Elect,

How are you this month? I hope that these letters have been beneficial to you. This is already the eleventh letter I've written to you. It was my intention, when I started writing these letters, to continue writing them for one year. It has really gone by quickly. I pray that God has been able to use these letters to encourage you in your Christian walk and in your relationship with your husband.

I know that the '80's has not been an easy decade in which to live as a Christian woman. Men and women are changing roles, divorce and immorality are on the rampage, and the traditional biblical role of a woman is demeaned and considered obsolete. We, now more than ever, need to be encouraged by the Word of God and by each other.

In Titus 2:4–5 the role of a Christian woman is defined. Paul wrote that the spiritually mature woman was to instruct the younger woman in her role. He did *not* tell them to encourage young women in any ministry or occupation other than that related to the home. He *didn't* tell them to teach the younger women to be evangelists, teachers, missionaries, career women, etc. He told them to teach women to be lovers of their husbands and their children. He told them to teach them to obey their husbands, to be domestic, clear thinking and pure.

Primarily, we as women are called to minister to our families. They are our mission field, with our husbands as our priority. As we abide in Christ, the fruits of the Spirit are produced in us for the benefit of our families. We can bestow on them God's love, joy, peace, mercy, etc. As we walk in the Spirit, in the role God has defined for a woman, we can also know that our rewards will be great in heaven. The rewards for a housewife on judgment day will be just as great as the rewards, for example, of a missionary, if this is where God has called her.

It is absolutely necessary for us to learn to live and walk in the Spirit of God just where we are. It is wrong to imagine that we would be happier, know God better, or be more effective as a Christian in a situation other than the one in which God has placed us. God has formed us as women in our mother's womb to be exactly *who* we are today. He chose our families, and the localities, and times in which we live. He has also permitted us to make the decisions in our lives that have led us to *where* we are today. If we desire to walk in the Spirit, it is necessary for us to accept God's plan for our lives. We must agree with it, walk in it and know it is God's will. There is always grace from God to walk in the will of God, and there is never grace for us if we resist His will.

In loving our husbands, raising our children, and taking care of our homes, we can walk in the fullness of God's Spirit and effect the world around us. In John 14:21 Jesus said that, if we obey Him, He will manifest Himself to us. He will manifest Himself to us, as women, as we obediently submit to the role in which He called us. I have found that, as a woman, I can know God through my domestic duties in life.

God is so near to each one of us, and He longs to fellowship with us. Christ died for us so that nothing could stand between us and constant communion with Him. As we look to Him, the everyday chores in a woman's life gain eternal value. As we commit these duties to God, we can grow to maturity in the soil in which God has planted us.

I urge you to make God's Word your priority in life. We do not "live by bread alone, but by every word that proceeds from the mouth of God (Matt. 4:4.)" His Word will nourish us, so we can continue to grow into the Godly women He intends us to be.

Love,

Judy

Scripture references:

• Titus 2:4-5 So that they may encourage the young women to love their husbands, to love their children, to *be* sensible, pure, workers at home, kind, being subject to their own husbands, so that the word of God will not be dishonored.

• John 14:21 "He who has My commandments and keeps them is the one who loves Me; and he who loves Me will be loved by My Father, and I will love him and will disclose Myself to him."

• Matthews 4:4 But He answered and said, "It is written, 'MAN SHALL NOT LIVE ON BREAD ALONE, BUT ON EVERY WORD THAT PROCEEDS OUT OF THE MOUTH OF GOD.'"

June 1989

Letter 11 ~ Questions

- What are some promises God has made to a woman who embraces the doctrine of submission?

- How has this study affected your marriage?

- How has your understanding of submission changed?

Dear Lady Elect,

You probably don't know me. I'm Judy's husband. I wanted to write this last letter to encourage you not to give up on your husband. I know he really needs you even though he probably wouldn't admit it. I know this because without Judy's faith and love I wouldn't have made it.

I was backslidden for seven years and did everything you could imagine. Judy believed in me when I didn't believe in myself anymore. She kept loving me and giving me grace even when I knew I didn't deserve it.

It looked like I was enjoying my sinful life, but I was under so much conviction that I prayed every night that I wouldn't wake up in the morning.

God is so faithful that on one of those mornings I woke up a new man and I knew that it was finally over. God had completely restored me. So, don't give up on your husband. If you do, he might not make it. He needs you. I know!

Love,

Dan

Made in the USA
Middletown, DE
30 June 2022

67559712R00045